Int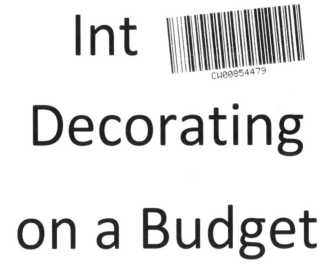

Decorating

on a Budget

A Budget Friendly Guide to Creating a
Home Which Makes You Truly Feel "at
Home" and Happy

By Matt McKinney

circumstances is the author responsible for any losses, direct or indirect, which are incurred as a result of the use of information contained within this document, including, but not limited to, —errors, omissions, or inaccuracies.

Contents

Thank you for buying this book and I hope that you will find it useful. If you will want to share your thoughts on this book, you can do so by leaving a review on the Amazon page, it helps me out a lot.

Introduction

Everybody wishes to decorate their home extravagantly, however, not everybody can afford luxurious prices. The bright side is you can construct and create a spectacular and well-designed home regardless of your budget. This guide is going to assist you produce an exceptional interior for your home that is going to ultimately end up being your sanctuary. Are you prepared to experience interior decoration without investing heaps of cash?

You landed in simply the appropriate place to find out everything you require to understand to furnish your home, regardless of your budget. Before you discover how to furnish your home, let us initially explore some misconceptions individuals have when it pertains to interior decoration. Comprehending and conquering these misconceptions, having the capability to tell the truth from fiction, is what eventually leads to success as you work to develop the home of your dreams.

Myth Buster

Interior decoration is not as tough as it might appear, however, there are individuals that might lead you to think that it is. Anybody can take pleasure in basic decorating tasks to improve the beauty of their house, whether new or refurbished. You do not need to spend a great deal of cash to produce an exceptional interior for your home. This is the primary misconception individuals believe when they consider interior decoration.

A few of the most lovely homes are decorated and designed with easy, practical and stunning things. Are you somebody that has fallen victim to this misconception? Learn precisely what is and is not true when it pertains to interior decoration, so you could develop a comfy, personal and properly designed house.

The pointers and ideas provided in this guide are appropriate for those thinking about decorating a brand-new house, or for those thinking about improving the feel and look of the home they currently have. When thinking about decorating on a minimal budget, there are particular truths you must quickly separate from fiction.

Here are some essential "truths" you ought to understand:

You could enhance the ambiance of any space in your house without spending a fortune. Interior decoration is quickly achieved even when you have little or no cash to invest. In some cases, it includes merely reorganizing the products and things in your house.

You do not need to have any experience with interior decorating to enhance the feel and look of your house. Many folks understand intuitively how to enhance the appearance of their house. I am going to teach you how to do this while dealing with a budget plan, so you could have whatever you desire, without going broke.

You can boost the worth of your house by enhancing a couple of areas of your house cheaply. You can utilize a couple of basic tools and strategies to develop a more flourishing living environment. You are going to discover this during this book.

You do need to set a budget plan when decorating, or you are going to spend excessive cash since, honestly, interior decoration is enjoyable! I am going to teach you how to set a proper budget plan later on in this book. When you produce your budget plan, adhere to it, and you are going to develop the home of your dreams.

This book is going to show you how to embellish any space in your house without spending a fortune. Whether you have $200 to invest or $10,00 to invest, you can utilize any of the suggestions in this guide to brighten the rooms in your house.

Bear in mind that the term "budget plan" suggests something different for everybody. The bright side is that this book supplies information for individuals that desire a superiorly designed interior despite their budget plan. All of the ideas, techniques and tools supplied in this guide are for individuals thinking about interior decoration without investing a fortune. There are certain ideas you could elaborate on and invest more cash on if you have the appropriate budget plan. Or, you could permit yourself to delight in the easy techniques and strategies in this book and utilize any additional cash you have on special treats for yourself or your household.

You are going to discover decorating suggestions that cost nothing, and some which might cost a couple of hundred or thousand dollars. Choose the pointers which coincide with your budget plan, and you are going to discover it simpler than you think to create the interior of your home quickly and entirely.

Are you all set to find out more? Then what are we waiting for? In the following area, you are going to take the initial essential action towards enhancing the look of your house. You are going to discover how to evaluate your house and recognize locations of your home that require the most enhancement. If you are dealing with a brand-new home, you might have to think about embellishing one room at a time.

If you intend to embellish an existing home, you could utilize the ideas laid out in the next area to identify the rooms in your home needing the most attention.

Home analysis is distinct for everybody. The actions described in the following area apply whether you reside in a duplex, little home or big compound. Ensure you read this part completely, so you can produce a plan for success when preparing to decorate the your home interio on a budget plan.

Chapter 1: Analyzing Your Home

Before you can start any task, you initially need to look at your home and assess what is crucial for you to create or revamp. If you do have a tight budget plan, you may wish to focus your efforts on a couple of living areas of your house. As soon as you have more cash to deal with, you could constantly return and decorate other spots of your home.

Certain individuals find interior decorating to be a lifelong procedure...

You might discover you spend time redecorating your home during your life. That is one reason you wish to decorate within a budget plan, so you do not wind up spending a lot throughout the procedure. When assessing your home, you ought to take an unbiased view of your home. In some cases, this includes asking someone else to go through your home with you and suggest spots that require improvement.

Eventually, you are going to choose what parts of your home to enhance. Often, nevertheless, you are going to find that working with somebody might lead to useful recommendations (like including shelving to decrease clutter). You might even discover a buddy that has experience with interior decoration. Working with a buddy when assessing your house is much less costly than working with somebody you pay to decorate or assess your home.

Common Sense Techniques

When you assess your home, you are taking stock of the things or elements of your home that you enjoy, and those you wish to alter. As you go through your home, it is necessary you use a common sense approach. Have a pen and paper nearby, and ensure you make a note of any ideas. For every room of your home you intend to decorate, you could produce different notes on different pages.

That manner in which you approach interior decorating utilizing sound judgement and useful, arranged approaches. Now, there are 2 methods to approach analysis. If you evaluate a brand-new residence, you are going to approach assessment from an "entire house" viewpoint, attempting to get the most bang for your buck. If you wish to enhance the feel and look of your present home, you can still evaluate your whole home, but might invest more time focusing on a couple of rooms in your home you know require the most attention.

The New Home Method

Evaluating your home is simple if you are working to decorate a brand-new home. Take every area separately and find what the most essential locations are for you to concentrate on. As discussed above, whether decorating for a brand-new home or for an existing one, you need to constantly approach interior decorating on a budget plan by concentrating your attention on a couple of rooms at a time.

When you purchase a brand-new home, you are going to need to evaluate what things you currently have which you can utilize in your home (such as beds or couches) and what things you have to purchase to finish your house. If, for instance, you relocate to a bigger home, you might have to purchase some extra furniture for included rooms in your home. When dealing with a budget plan, you might utilize what you have already, and decorate rooms separately, one room at a time. If you attempt to decorate simultaneously, you might discover that you invest too much cash and too much time fretting about budgeting. Take a couple of rooms, and turn them into the focus of your work.

Remodeling an Existing Home

Many folks organize their plans and schedules to decorate based upon the rooms for which they feel that they require the most assistance. Typically individuals wish to decorate a single room in the home. Others might choose a grouping of rooms, such as the bedrooms, or a single bedroom to remodel or decorate for a new arrival (such as an infant).

For certain individuals, the rooms they concentrate on are the ones individuals are most probable to see on visiting. For instance, you might wish to improve the look of your foyer or living room. Others wish to enhance the functionality of rooms, such as the kitchen area. Maybe you desire more space in your kitchen area so you may cook, but likewise entertain company. You might wish to spruce up your kitchen area so it appears bigger if you do not have sufficient counter area. Ensure that, as you walk through the rooms you wish to concentrate on, you take notes of what things are crucial for you to change.

Keep in mind, as you go through a home and begin evaluating it, you might reconsider what is important. You might wish to enhance the appearance of your bedroom, or design a brand-new bedroom for a brand-new infant entering your life. Whatever you wish to do, the secret to your success is having a budget plan. This applies whether you deal with an existing home, or whether you intend to embellish a brand-new home. The budget plan ought to be the base for all choices regarding interior decorating. Your budget plan is going to assist you choose what things you need to purchase, and what products you can decorate with little fanfare or attention. You might choose to start some DIY tasks so you save cash and could invest cash in areas that require the most attention.

Interior decorating could be costly; however, not if you take a logical approach.

In some cases, a few of the best homes you see are those which utilize common sense decorating approaches. Common sense starts with the analysis of your home and developing a budget plan to work with. Always remember that. Never ever step away from your budget, or you might discover you plunge into debt.

Tips on Setting a Budget

You establish a budget plan by initially choosing what rooms you have to decorate. You do this when you complete evaluating your home. After you make your notes, take a seat and choose what areas of your home you wish to focus on.

If you are having a brand-new infant or have an addition to your house, this is simple. You are going to likely choose these rooms to decorate initially. If you plan to decorate numerous rooms, this could be a tad tougher but definitely possible. You are going to just have to find out how to prioritize your interior decoration, and find out how to create an interior without investing a lot.

So initially, set a budget plan. How do you do that, right?

The response is easy. Learn just how much cash you have available for decorating.

Consider when setting your budget plan your month-to-month earnings, your expenses, and just how much cash you are able to afford to invest in decorating without guilt and boosting your debt-to-income ratio. Meaning, you wish to stay away from entering into debt merely by decorating your home. So find out how much cash you need to play with. Jot this number down, due to the fact that you are going to refer back to it frequently when choosing instruments to decorate your home with.

When producing a budget plan, you might discover a couple of items you wish to charge. This is ok, simply make certain you are able to pay for those things in a short time. In case you charge excessively when decorating, you might wind up paying 10 times more for decoration than you wished to. Keep in mind all charge cards bring rates of interest. Unless you are able to pay off what you charge in a month, think hard and long prior to considering your credit balance as portion of your budget plan.

After producing a budget plan, follow these steps to assist you to evaluate your home's requirements:

Focus on the rooms you wish to decorate. Label every room. When the time comes to decorate, you are going to begin with space at the top of the list. You might halt there up until you have more cash to deal with other rooms, or move to another space if you still have a bit of extra money. You might discover, by utilizing the pointers in this book, you are able to decorate all the spaces in your house to your heart's desire. It all depends upon your budget plan, and just how much time you wish to spend on DIY projects.

Identify just how much cash you have available to utilize for interior decoration. You established your spending plan when determining your costs for the month. If you have numerous rooms to decorate, think about spliting your budget plan by the number of spaces you wish to decorate. You might then designate slightly less or more to spaces that require more assistance than others. For instance, you might wish to invest more cash when decorating the dining or living areas as opposed to the bathroom.

Make a list of the spaces you can decorate based upon your budget plan in the immediate future. Often the room you focus on as # 1 might be too pricey to decorate in the short-run. Attempt to make small modifications, and choose another top-priority room to decorate which fits within your present budget plan. If you have just one room, utilize the cash you do have to furnish the room as much as you are able to by utilizing the ideas offered in this book. Begin with high-priority things. You can constantly decorate your room additionally when you have more money.

Make certain you keep in mind items you have currently that you can refurbish to enhance the feel and look of your home, and products you have to replace or purchase brand-new (as when it comes to a brand-new room or home). Anything you can refurbish is going to most likely cost less than items you should purchase brand-new. In some cases, you need to reassess any presumptions you have regarding what interior decorating is or is not. Keep in mind, the objective here is to produce a fresh look for the rooms in your house without spending a ton of money. This might need a bit of hands-on work. You might discover you like and delight in the procedure, many people find it extremely restorative. As soon as you end up decorating your rooms, you can feel happy you contributed to creating the atmosphere you have.

When you established a budget plan, spend a bit of time time shopping around and going through the concepts in this book. If you discover you just have ample cash to work on a couple of spaces, begin your own design "savings" jar. This is absolutely nothing more than a jar you could stash a tiny amount of cash away in for a couple of months, to spare for your following decorating extravaganza. Ensure you do not take cash out of this jar. In case you feel lured to do so, then establish a closed bank account where you are punished for taking out your savings prematurely. Saving for interior decoration is just like retirement saving. You wish to stash away your cash carefully and securely, and just make use of it when the time arrives to do that without penalty.

Often, a bit of extra change is all it requires ...

Some individuals collect extra change to pay for a night out. If you wish to decorate your home, save your extra change for that. Have a piggy bank filled with coins, and you are going to discover before you know it that you have simply the correct amount of cash to spend for what you require.

Now is time to carry on to the enjoyable part. You understand what rooms you wish to embellish, you have a budget plan. Now is the time to choose what kind of individual you are, and what styles you wish your home to show. Many homes reflect the character and preferences of the owner. Make certain you spend time evaluating your own preferences, so during decorating, you choose what you are happy with.

Styles

It is essential when evaluating your home that you think about the styles which dominate your home. Learn what you enjoy about your home, and what you feel you need to change to be more "at home" in your home. If you lately purchased a house, you might discover you wish to change the whole interior. There is absolutely nothing wrong with this, simply make certain you invest ample time assessing your house and your preferences prior to making adjustments.

You do not wish to squander cash and time purchasing country-themed décor just to discover later you much prefer a more modern styled home.

Remember, when doing this, certain styles or themes might consist of more costly accessories than others, but for the most part, regardless of your style or preference, you may find methods to decorate your home even on a strict budget plan.

How do you choose a theme for your home? Consider the homes you go to and what you enjoy about them, as this is going to offer you an idea about what kind of individual you are and what designs you like the most. Think about checking out a couple of interior decoration mags so you may distinguish between modern, contemporary, country, art deco and other designs.

You must likewise inventory your furnishings and home, as they might supply some insight into your preferences and style.

For instance, do you like a modern feel and look? Are you trendy? Or maybe you prefer a more classic or vintage home. Others prefer a country appearance, while still others prefer a well balanced home styled in numerous manners.

The kinds of decorations you decorate your home with are going to ultimately reflect your character and design preferences, so this is an essential step when setting a budget.

When you pick the theme of your home, you are going to have a much better grasp of what areas of your house require the most attention when it pertains to decorating and altering the present appearance of your home. Possibly, for instance, the majority of your home has a modern appearance and design, however, you find your dining area is more contemporary or traditional. You might likewise wish to create a home which is more useful. If your home is more ornamental than you want, you may alter that. Simply make certain you understand what you desire before you begin making changes.

You may wish to alter the appearance of your dining area by including a couple of pieces or altering the furniture to show the design which encompasses the remainder of your home. You might wish to create a kitchen area which has open space and higher utility to move within.

Do not believe, nevertheless, that you need to design your home in one precise way. Some individuals choose to embellish their homes in numerous styles. Your living area, for instance, might reflect a country-like beauty, while your kitchen area might look like a country pad. While it is simpler to stick to one style, eventually, you choose what you desire (and do not want) your home to appear like. You might find it enjoyable to blend and match when decorating. This frequently works great with couples who have different preferences when it pertains to themes and styles. Work with your partner when choosing how you wish to decorate specific rooms. You could each take charge of a room so you both feel involved in the decorating procedure.

Tip

Ensure you create a list of essential things before you begin decorating. Certain things you might find you can't live without ...

For some people, these might consist of couches, beds, tables and so forth. For others, essential must-haves can consist of artwork or plants. Must-haves are things which help you feel complete, but also are essential for you to feel comfy in your home.

If you have the fundamentals and just require things to complement the feel and look of your home, you are going to find decorating a breeze.

In the following part, we are going to discuss a couple of basic things you may do to enhance the atmosphere in your home without spending a bunch of cash. The entire purpose of this book is, besides, to teach you HOW to decorate without spending excessively. You are simply a step away from finding out all there is to understand ...

Chapter 2: Make Small Changes Initially

If you wish to be successful at interior decorating on a budget plan, you should think small. The majority of people think that to be effective at interior decorating, they need to make remarkable changes to their whole living area. This very rarely holds true. In fact, wise decorators are those who take on tasks which are little initially, before proceeding to substantial undertakings.

In some cases, tiny changes are all that is required to make a huge difference in your home's look.

In this part, you are going to find out about certain basic steps and concepts you could take to enhance your home's look. When you take the steps detailed in this part, you might find that you can redecorate your home without investing a single cent. Odds are high you are going to invest some cash. However, you can enhance the feel and look of your house by making changes which need time, not cash.

You might find after embracing a few of the changes in this part, you need not alter your home any more. Decorating on a budget plan could be as complicated or easy as you desire. Attempt to streamline your life, and you are going to find that ending up being an effective interior decorator is the simplest job on the planet.

Here are a couple of tiny ways to make significant differences in how your home feels and looks.

Tiny Changes to Enhance Existing Rooms

1. Think about including wallpaper to a room which requires a bit of sprucing up. You could likewise utilize wall-border, which is much less costly, to decorate the upper or lower sides of a wall. At the same time, you could develop borders by stenciling or painting designs on your walls, or by getting rid of existing borders to provide a room with a new appearance or feel.

2. Locate some mirrors and put them in areas in your home where they reflect light. This is going to make the room you put the mirrors in seem bigger. Your home is going to likewise appear as if it gets more sunshine. Do not put mirrors throughout your home in locations where they detract from the room's look, or in places where they reflect unappealing things (such as your driveway or garage) unless you actually desire this.

3. Attempt restoring antiques or old furniture instead of purchasing brand-new furniture, which might be pricey, but not nearly as important as your used thing. You may do this cheaply with the aid of a neighborhood Home Depot or home improvement shop. You might have to finish and sand, then stain a cabinet, for instance, to enhance its look. In instances where you have to cover water stains, you might think about positioning a strategically positioned crocheted fabric or another ornamental thing, like a lamp.

4. Cover stains up instead of re-carpeting your home. You do not need to pay a stain removal expert to enhance the look of your carpet. A lot of individuals have spots on their carpet, and many find a method to decorate over them without investing a fortune. Let's face it. Many times, when a stain exists, it is difficult to eliminate, regardless of how much you clean it. You might wash it so that it seems to disappear, just to find it comes back a couple of weeks later on. Thankfully, no stain is impossible to conceal. And conceal it you will IF you wish to save cash. The majority of bargain interior decorators strategically utilize furniture and toss rugs to conceal hard-to-remove spots. If you have kids, purchase some affordable remnants to put over your home so you could quickly get rid of and clean them if they end up being stained.

5. Attempt allowing more light in your home. If you have curtains, get rid of them. Attempt blinds, or attempt a bare window. Simply make certain you keep your window tidy. You might wish to stencil or paint on the window utilizing paints you can discover at any hobby shop. This produces the result of stained glass, without spending the cash. Some individuals

discover they could utilize stick-on appliqués on a bare window to produce the look of stained glass. These appliqués are affordable, and you could typically discover them online. They are a fantastic tool for decorating kids' rooms, as many can be found in cartoon styles.

6. Think about including some plants or a little, economical fountain in your home to bring in a subtle atmosphere and relaxing appeal. In case you do not have a green thumb, choose something that is simple to grow, and sturdy, such as a bamboo tree (some think this even brings prosperity to luck and your home). You do not need to purchase a thousand dollar fountain. Attempt getting a little yet appealing $15 fountain online. Toss some rocks in it and let it go. You might find you feel more peaceful in your home. Fountains are additionally extremely beneficial for enhancing the atmosphere of a home office.

7. Utilize fabrics to assist enhance the feel and look of worn-out furnishings. Fabric shops sell gorgeous slipcovers and fabrics cheaply. Far more economical is it to utilize a cover or to recover an existing couch than to purchase a brand-new one. If you are not handy with a thread and needle, search for slipcovers that can immediately alter the feel and look of your couch (and even hide stains).

8. Attempt painting several of the walls in your room or in numerous areas in your home to offer your house a clean slate. You could purchase paint cheaply, and you do not need to hire an expert painter to do the work (though you could locate some college students that are handy at painting, who are probable to charge less than "expert" painters). Utilize light and brilliant colors for rooms you take pleasure in throughout the day, and soothing colors such as dark green or blue for rooms you wish to kick back in. Make certain the colors you pick match the furniture you have or the upholstery you utilize in your home. Certain individuals find excellent painting is all they require to embellish their homes in a brand-new and significant way.

9. Try utilizing lamps without any shades, or decorate plain shades you have at home. This is going to include intensity and color to any area. You can purchase colored bulbs that include an intriguing feel and look to practically any room, and make any lamp appear terrific rather than lacking when you do not utilize a shade.

10.   Utilize even more paint to make a mural on a wall or a sponge you dipped in the paint to include texture to a wall's surface. You could practice this beforehand by using the paint to a piece of old wood, or a wall you intend to repaint anyhow. There are limitless ways to decorate utilizing paint, so offer the paint a shot. Do not just consider paint as a thing to utilize as a cover for a whole wall. Consider it an accessory where possible. Some individuals, for instance, purchase low-cost stencils and furnish the walls of an area in their home by administering paint to the stencils. This is specifically enjoyable for a kid's playroom or room, where you could stencil paint your kid's name, the letters of the alphabet or cool numbers.

Keep in mind, small changes typically make a huge impression on you and individuals visiting your home. Begin little, see what you think. If you wish to carry on, you can.

Now that you understand what it requires to alter a little room or part of your home, let us now take a bit of time to assess change on a much bigger scale. Keep in mind, even while making huge changes to the within your home, this book is all about budgeting.

Some individuals discover, nevertheless, after carrying out some tiny changes, that they change the list they created when initially prioritizing how they felt their home needs to look. In case you find the small changes you make suffice to produce a visually enticing environment, you might choose only one huge change, your "high-ticket" thing, or you might choose to stick to small changes forever, so you could decorate the whole interior of your home. Keep in mind, the choice is yours. The lesson to learn is to begin little.

Beginning small is going to additionally develop your skills and ability to make bigger changes when the time is proper. You might find you can postpone making bigger changes for a number of years when you make a couple of changes to enhance the look of your house.

Now is the time to discover how to create a huge difference in the way one space or numerous rooms in your house appear without investing a fortune. While we have actually spent a great deal of time discussing how fantastic tiny changes are (and they are), there are times when big changes are truly what you need to furnish your home.

Some refer to this procedure as the home "makeover." We have actually all seen the programs on tv, where individuals have $3,000 and need to redecorate a whole home, supplying it a brand-new, fresh face. You could do the identical thing, and spend even less cash.

Ready to discover how? Then carry on to the following chapter.

Chapter 3: Taking The Plunge

In some cases, tiny changes are insufficient to produce the remarkable changes you desire in your home. You understand this, we drilled the point into your head. Often, huge changes are likewise beneficial. You might discover after living in a house for several years, that you require a makeover. In some cases, you discover that your home requires a make-under. I am going to teach you how to carry out both, without spending excessively or too little.

There are individuals who work with budget plans which are big enough to pay for total overhauls of several rooms in the house utilizing any method they desire. If this holds true, the ideas in this part are going to aid you to decorate on a bigger scale without spending a lot. You can utilize all the cash you save for a great vacation. Keep in mind, even if doing a total makeover, there is no reason you need to spend a ton of money when decorating your house.

How do you complete a whole makeover when working on a budget plan? The response is easy ... goal setting.

Goal Setting

You already realize how essential it is for you to inventory your home prior to decorating, and how crucial it is to budget prior to decorating. When you achieve these 2 feats, you can then set goals showing your requirements and viewpoints, your desires and wants for your home.

You could establish short or long-term goals for your home. Total overhauls of your whole home are feasible, specifically when you establish short, medium and long-term goals. By carrying this out, you develop a timeline for finishing your home's interior décor.

Great Goal Setting

Great goal setting is extremely crucial for your success as a budget interior decorator. Your goals ought to reflect the modifications you wish to make and fit inside your budget plan.

Every goal you set needs to be economical, workable and achievable. Here are certain instances of great goals you could set when preparing to revamp your home:

1. Eliminate all old wallpaper in the front room within 2 weeks

2. Review colors and paints at the neighborhood home improvement shop by following Wednesday.

3. Look for discount bamboo flooring on the 23rd.

4. Re-stain and finish the exterior deck prior to the conclusion of the summer season

5. Locate throw rugs for all stains on the carpet by early Fall

6. Paint the kitchen area and great room by the end of Spring

All these goals are workable. They all consist of particular things (such as painting or getting rid of wallpaper) and a timeframe for finishing the job.

Setting goals is great when you understand you can accomplish them. The only way you have to determine whether you are successful is by assessing what progress you are making. You do this by setting times of the year or dates you wish to have particular interior decorating projects commenced or finished by.

You might discover that as you make tiny modifications to your home, your goals alter gradually, yet steadily. As you reach specific goals, you might include brand-new objectives or goals to your list.

When setting goals, attempt to prioritize your goals and line them up with the rooms you focus on for decorating or refurbishing in your home. For instance, if you plan a total overhaul of your home, yet wish to begin with the living room, your short-term goals must consist of the actions you have to take to enhance the look of this area.

As soon as you attain these goals, you may carry on to other appropriate goals. Develop brand-new ones, so the creative process never ever stops.

As soon as you have your goals in place, you may move to the following action, which is investigating the materials you are going to require to attain your goals. When examining the devices and tools you require, you want to think about the quality of the material in addition to your cost.

Normally, you can discover quality materials without paying high prices, you simply need to find out how to search for them. Many people rely on the Web when trying to find products or items to decorate their home. You are going to likewise discover that lots of neighborhood retailers and house improvement shops typically provide specials on select products throughout numerous times of the year. Have your eyes and ears open for these specials so you are able to make the most of them.

You could always look for clearance items, and stock up on them so when the time arrives to remodel, you have all you require, and you just spent the cash you planned to spend by sticking to your budget plan. Here are certain added ideas for purchasing the things you require to decorate your home on a bigger-scale, without spending way too much cash.

Purchasing Products to Decorate Your Home

If you intend to furnish your home's interior, you are going to have to purchase supplies to do this appropriately. These supplies might consist of a tool kit, wood flooring, wallpaper, glue ...

The key to an effective transition on a budget plan is organization. If you make a list of products you require to accomplish your goals one room at a time, you are going to save cash, and stay clear of paying cash for supplies you discover you do not require. You are not going to make it through if you just begin making changes without considering how to make changes wisely. Keep in mind, you need to create a blueprint for success. Set out everything you wish to alter in your home before you make any modifications, and after that, go all out.

How do you know which supplies you require? Assess the changes you wish to make to a room. If you intend to paint a room, for instance, you are going to require various supplies than if you intend to wallpaper a room. Considering that painting is among the least pricey methods to decorate, let us spend a bit of time speaking about interior painting and manners in which you may purchase low-cost paint for your home.

Painting on a Budget plan

Painting a wall or your whole home is an easy and affordable method to decorate. You do not need to paint all the areas in your home to include ambiance and beauty to your home. Actually, many people on a budget plan begin with one room, and ultimately work their way up to decorating their whole home. You might find that painting one wall makes a significant distinction in how your home appears. Attempt it, allow it to sit for a while, and after that, paint a bit more if you feel you have to.

When you choose what room or rooms you wish to paint (or which walls require paint) you should purchase appropriate tools. You do not wish to purchase unneeded items. Always try to find the ideal paint, but not the most costly. Paint is just as a bottle of fine wine. A few of the ideal wines are not the most pricey wines, but not the cheapest either. Typically, they fall someplace in between the two extremes.

Say, for instance, you wish to paint your living room, and put a bit of artwork on the walls. To attain thcsc goals, you might require:

A drop cloth or other product to catch paint which falls from brushes or rollers while you paint. You could purchase a formal cloth, or utilize big blankets you have no other usage for and do not mind spilling paint on as long as the paint will not leak through to the floor. Certain individuals choose coating the floors with plastic initially and after that a drop cloth of some kind. You might discover a secondhand drop cloth at a yard sales. The identical holds true of wall hangings for your freshly painted home.

Purchase indoor paint and perhaps a protective coating, to assist stop cracking or damage to your walls. In case you are unsure what kind of paint you require, ask a professional at your neighborhood interior decoration or home improvement shop. You could pick from numerous paint textures and colors. Many come with integrated lacquers or chip-proof components that are going to save you cash. Typically you are going to discover you do not have to purchase the most pricey paint to get great paint. Ask a professional to refer you to the ideal paint you are able to get within the budget plan you have. You can likewise look into the kind of paint you must purchase online. You might discover it less costly to buy paint online after talking to a professional at your local home improvement shop.

Paint brushes or rollers. Here is an additional instance of an item you wish to purchase that is of fine quality. Nevertheless, your brushes and roller do not need to be the most pricey on the marketplace.

Hooks or nails for hanging wall fixtures, unless you already have a supply readily available. You might likewise require a hammer.

A ladder if you intend to paint ceilings, or other tough-to-reach places. If you are not comfy utilizing a ladder, make certain you have somebody with you to steady the ladder as you utilize it.

Tape you could utilize to cover the borders beneath your wall so you do not mistakenly spill paint on them. You could discover the appropriate type of tape at most home improvement shops. You desire a tape that is not going to leave a sticky film on your walls, but the tape that is more powerful than scotch tape. "Painters" tape is all you need to ask for.

You might require other supplies depending upon the kind of painting you wish to do. If you intend to decorate over paint by using stencils or by utilizing the sponge painting method, you are going to require different supplies. Once again, do your research. Look for some guidance from a professional at your neighborhood paint or home-improvements shop. They are going to tell you what you require. Make certain you purchase just what you require, and not the extras they might attempt to offer you.

If you are unable to purchase all you require, learn if you have buddies or family members that might have a few of the supplies you desire, and ask to borrow them. A lot of them are going to be more than pleased to aid, and might even help you paint.

Painting Tips To Save You Money And Time

If you paint instead of hiring somebody to paint, you are going to save a great deal of cash. You do wish for your home to appear stylish, however, if you intend to paint, it is necessary you do it properly.

Here are several suggestions to guarantee you paint properly even if you have no experience painting.

-Always utilize a plastic cloth referred to as a drop cloth to shield your carpets or floors from dripping paint. I understand I've pointed this out previously, however, you would be shocked at how many individuals fail to utilize a correct cloth. You are going to spend more cash getting paint spots out of your carpet than you are going painting your walls if you are not cautious.

-Cover your paint can with plastic or place on a cardboard surface so the paint does not drip from your paint can onto your floor. You do not, besides, wish to spend additional cash purchasing items to get rid of spilled paint.

-Cover your shoes and other pieces of clothing to protect against paint spots. You could utilize basic shower caps or plastic bags to shield your shoes, and choose a worn out or damaged set of jeans and a t-shirt to utilize for painting tasks. Make certain you take the covers off your shoes prior to walking around the remainder of your house, so you do not spread out paint to floors in other areas.

-If you intend to paint the ceiling, do this initially. In case you do not, the paint may drip to your walls.

-As you are painting, constantly paint from high to low, in order to aid to avoid unneeded dripping. If you slip up, do not worry, cover it and have a go at it again.

-Tape around electrical outlets (and get rid of the covering) to prevent paint leakage. You could likewise put tape around moldings to aid to protect against unexpected spills.

-Fill in any holes in your walls unless you intend to hang a picture in the precise spot you paint over. You may do this quickly with a small "spackle" available at practically every home improvement shop. You might discover that you are able to borrow some from a neighbor or buddy, if you wish to save cash and do not wish to purchase a whole can.

-Utilize a guide when required. If, for instance, you intend to paint a dark wall light, utilize a lighter color to paint over the dark color to prepare or prime your wall, so the color you choose ends up how you want it to look.

You might wish to attempt painting a little room initially before proceeding to bigger projects. The more practice you receive, the better you are going to be at painting. Some individuals take time out of their day to follow expert painters as they do their task. You may consider this, specifically if you know somebody who paints good. Or, you might know a professional painter who might utilize a few of your services, and offer a trade, so you save cash.

For instance, you might offer to do their taxes if they paint your home interior. Simply make certain if you do go into agreements such as this, you always sign an agreement so you stay away from unneeded fights about who settled on what. You must likewise ensure you set a deadline for all work to be finished by. This aids to protect against arguments.

If you are still uncertain about what you require, check in with the professionals. Here are certain fantastic resources for information on what kinds of paints to purchase and accessories if you intend to decorate your home cheaply. By looking into these websites, you are going to save cash on a pricey consultant or professional estimate of your requirements.

Keep in mind there are countless resources you could check out regarding painting. You could even purchase books which show you how to paint well, or take classes. Lots of home improvement shops hold workshops which last anywhere from an hour to a day, and the majority of are less costly even after you purchase the paint, rather than hiring an expert painter to do the task for you.

The more time you devote to preparing, the more cash you are going to save.

Total Home Makeovers Extras

Many people wish to do more than paint when they prepare for a total makeover for their home. Thankfully, you could still accomplish this with your budget. You need to plan for these extra changes and include them into your makeover plan.

In this segment, we are going to speak about how to save cash when it comes to numerous areas of your home. You might even discover that you develop your own extraordinary ideas after reading a few of the useful suggestions and tools offered.

Many topics are covered to aid to provide the most information possible on nearly any kind of improvement you might make to your home. The suggestions offered are for individuals on any budget, however, they are going to spare cash for everybody utilizing them.

Circle the ideas or jot down the ideas you believe are going to work ideally for your home after evaluating this list. You might choose to combine a few of these with a brand-new paint task to decorate your home as you want it.

Tips for Flooring Improvement

One easy way to alter your home's look is to deal with bad flooring. Individuals with carpeted floors typically fall under 2 classifications; they do not enjoy their carpets' color or their carpets are stained and worn out.

No matter your scenario, you do not have to pay cash to have brand-new wall-to-wall carpeting set up to repair the appearance of your carpet and enhance your home's interior. You could purchase throw rugs to conceal spots on your carpet. Lots of folks place furniture over worn carpet areas.

There is this thing that you must not place carpet over carpet among some individuals. This is a misconception, so ignore it. There is no reasoning supporting this misconception. Actually, lots of home improvement shops offer specialized items to keep a throw rug from wrinkling if put atop the carpet. You might discover remnants you can likewise utilize to toss over your carpet at any carpet outlet.

If you have hardwood floors yet do not have the cash to have them refinished, think about purchasing an economical and big throw rug or more to enhance the look of your flooring. Lots of carpets are quickly laundered in a big washer, so you do not need to pay pricey dry cleaners for cleaning

In case you go to a standard store to purchase carpets or throw rugs, you are going to discover that they are really pricey. Rather, head to eBay.com or other auction websites and see if anybody is offering oriental rugs or comparable pieces such as carpet-runners, which you could put throughout your home. Search for those with minimal wear and tear. These are products you can change whenever you wish to offer your house a fresh look. You could even alter them seasonally to enhance the atmosphere in your home.

You could likewise check out ethnic or little novelty stores due to the fact that they frequently offer hand-woven rugs extremely cheaply (surprisingly). You could get a throw rug created from soft wool or comparable materials to cover nearly the whole surface of a little room for $100 in many cases.

You could likewise take a look at second-hand shops for used carpets or yard sale. One person's trash might be another's treasure. Here are a couple of additional ideas for enhancing the feel and look of your floors:

Utilize dim lighting if you wish to conceal spots or a worn carpet. Absolutely nothing makes a stain stick out more than direct exposure to the sun or intense light. Think of the lighting utilized in dressing rooms. It always makes us look our worst. Have compassion for your rugs and offer appropriate, reflective light.

Stay clear of exposing wood floors to straight sunshine or spills, as this might warp the material. In case you do spill anything on the floor, be sure to clean it right away with a dry fabric. Locate something to shade your floors if they are exposed to sunshine throughout particular times of the day.

Think about a "no shoe" rule in your house to keep your floors appearing fresher longer. Many people track in excessive dirt from outside when they wear their shoes within the home. You could have a set of slippers prepared to use in the home in case you like having your feet warm.

Concentrate on decorating other spots of your living space, and putting things up high on the walls so individuals are less probable to take a look at your flooring, and more probable to look at your tactically positioned plants, hangings or other things. For instance, you could put images throughout your home high above the flooring, so individuals instantly take a look at the pictures instead of staring at your floor. In case you have a big statue on the floor, you are going to draw attention to the floor. Once again, this is nothing more than a common sense suggestion to enhance the look of your home.

Consider snap-in "fake" hardwood flooring. Numerous home improvement shops sell DIY hardwood flooring. It might not be created from the identical material old-school flooring is. However, it could work similarly well. You could even purchase "snap-in" floor covering you actually snap into place, so you do not need to hire a pricey consultant to set your flooring up.

Remember that some flooring is cheaper than others; cork flooring for instance, and some kinds of bamboo flooring, include a lovely appearance and appeal to a home, and typically cost less than other hardwoods such as oak. They maintain the identical sturdiness and frequently last 20 or more years, so it deserves looking into. Do not purchase the most affordable items only, search for those which are durable and are going to last you a very long time. That way you do not need to stress over replacing them typically or ever, so you are going to save cash in the long-run. If you sell your home, you could include this to enhance your home's value.

Think about purchasing wood flooring which is not finished. You could stain and water seal the flooring on your own to spare cash. You could likewise ask a buddy to aid you to do this. This is another example where trading services is useful. And if you do not have a "trade" you could utilize as a bartering tool, get imaginative. Attempt offering somebody a night out, offer to look after their kids. You may discover you are amazed at how simple it is to get aid from others when you are kind, open and ready to ask.

My preferred method to improve the appearance of flooring without spending a lot is by utilizing runners in high traffic areas. Frequently you could purchase gorgeous runners, lengthy carpet stretches, really cheaply. Runners can be found in many various colors, designs and patterns. You are going to keep your floors and add to the design of your home.

Keep in mind, laminate and replica wood flooring items frequently look just as great if not better than the actual thing. They are simple to set up, and you are able to accessorize them cheaply with a couple of well-positioned throw rugs. These are an outstanding option for individuals that wish to improve their home interior without spending a lot on carpets.

Accessorizing Rooms with Hangings, lamps and More

Yet another method to decorate your home elegantly without spending a ton of money is to accessorize. The majority of people over-accessorize. If you wish to budget, search for a little selection of quality pieces and if anything, think about under-accessorizing your home. A couple of unique pieces well positioned in your home are going to prove a lot more intriguing than a house loaded with numerous inexpensive accessories.

Accessories consist of lamps, wall hangings, paintings, vases, plants and other things that can bring a sense of elegance and peace to an area or your home. You could likewise include things you create, including paintings, dream catchers or items your kids make at school (hang their artwork on the walls). Keep in mind, you wish to develop a home which offers appeal, yet one that likewise reflects your character. Put what you like out, and put your accessories in handy, attractive places.

You could likewise create a special appeal by choosing one recognized item and utilizing it as the focal point for the room you decorate. Simplicity is crucial if you intend to include a unique object in your home.

Let's say, for instance, you wish to decorate your dining area. You initially repaint the walls in a stylish color. You then have a dining room table purposefully positioned in the middle of the room. Pick one classy item as the focal point for your dining area. This might be a vase, for instance, which you fill with fresh flowers.

The tinted walls and focal point will be the things which stick out.

Suggestion For Dealing With Clutter

In some cases, the ideal way to enhance the look of your home and enable room for "decor" is to eliminate clutter. You can quickly acknowledge a clutter bug. They have stacks of paper piled atop the fridge.

Drawers filled with needless. Knickknacks throughout your home ... the list goes on. Rather than worrying, why not construct or purchase an affordable cabinet, one which is visually pleasing, and "keep" your clutter there?

This is an easy way to conceal clutter, which constantly makes an area or home appear 10 times better. Ultimately, if you have time, think about getting rid of as much clutter as you are able to. Some individuals stack their clutter in their garage. What takes place if you relocate to a little place? Attempt setting aside a day every month to look through and get rid of the clutter you have in your home. You are going to discover that you feel invigorated for doing so, and enhance your home's utility and look.

In case you have cabinets, you could always have them shined and refinished to aid them to look their finest, or perhaps add low-cost handles to enhance the feel and look of your cabinets. The majority of people instantly presume they need to switch out something that looks used. Extremely rarely is this the case. In fact, worn items which get a little TLC typically lend an extra appeal to a room since they are charming.

Keep in mind, when making over a home, typically less is more. It is the little details and the individual touches that individuals frequently notice. You can alter the lights in your home to incorporate beauty. You could change the fixtures on a used faucet to make it appear fresh. These little changes do not cost much, yet could make a huge difference.

The Main Three Changes Everybody Can Make

In this part, you are going to discover how 3 basic changes can change how you feel about your home in a single second. You could decorate your home quickly if you embrace even one of these concepts. You could utilize these changes to decorate an area or a whole home, even if they just have a little budget plan to deal with.

Initially, always buy the paint. Keep in mind, paint is the interior decorator's best buddy. You could utilize paint in numerous ways to enhance how your home looks.

Next, think about getting rid of clutter. You could actually remodel your whole home simply by getting rid of clutter. You might find it surprising simply just how much an uncluttered area means.

Last, include a couple of crucial pieces, such as the artwork you purchase at an auction, at a yard sale, or that you create yourself, to decorate an area or your home. Think about, for instance, family photos. You could sort through photos and make collages of members of the family to decorate your walls.

You could purchase low-cost wood frames and paint them to produce a distinct wall hanging for any area in your home. When it pertains to budget plan interior decorating, even when attempting to makeover your whole home, in some cases, basic changes are the ideal changes to make. One technique lots of people find extremely useful when interior decorating on a budget plan is Feng Shui. In the following part of this book, you are going to discover more about this ancient practice. Learn how to place it to use and save cash when decorating your house's interior, no matter the design or theme you pick for your home or living area.

Feng Shui On A Budget

Among the more prominent methods to decorate the interior of home nowadays is a method called Feng Shui. You could work with a pricey Feng Shui professional to decorate your house, or utilize the basic tools laid out within this book to create a well-decorated and tranquil home.

Feng Shui is not a mystical and magical system. It is an ancient, practical art meant to assist individuals in creating their living space in such a way which promotes positive energy and recovery. There are numerous easy principles you are able to embrace when decorating your home that are going to enhance the look of your home, and perhaps your health, luck wealth and success while at it.

The objective of Feng Shui consists of making a living space which is well balanced. Generally, homes decorated properly are well balanced, well designed and clutter-free. They are appealing on numerous levels to many individuals, which is why I chose to devote a whole chapter to the art of Feng Shui. Some essential factors to consider in Feng Shui consist of color, which lots of people believe has an impact on emotion, and "flow" or the balance of good energy.

You are going to find out more about each of these essential elements in the sections ahead.

Feng Shui and Color On A Budget Plan

Painting your walls is one method of decorating your home. The colors you pick can have an incredible effect on how you feel while in your home. Many individuals, including researchers, think color impacts individuals in various ways. If you wish to enhance how you feel AND embellish your home, you need to paint, but you likewise need to paint utilizing the appropriate colors. You want the colors you choose to bring out favorable feelings and emotions to generate balance.

How do you do that? You consider how color impacts your character, your spirit, and your dislike or like of a space or place in your home.

Some individuals, for instance, react to dark colors as relaxing and cool, while others find them anxiety-inducing or gloomy. It is necessary you acknowledge the common reactions related to numerous colors and discover how YOU respond to color prior to painting a room or area in your home.

Have you ever walked into a location where you felt really calm? Did you see the colors in the place? Begin taking notice of color as you go through your everyday activities. You might begin to see some colors trigger favorable reactions in you and others.

Lots of feel blue and green, for instance, are unwinding colors. Red frequently stimulates individuals, however, this is not always the case. Certain individuals feel the most calm when surrounded by deep, abundant colors.

Many individuals find intense colors annoying, so have this in mind when painting your home. Your home is going to be the location where you discover the greatest serenity, however, you are going to likely, likewise, welcome others into your home. The color in your room might establish the tone for your engagements and interactions with others.

Many folks find darker rooms tiring or depressing. This could be helpful if you wish to induce sleepiness, however, it is not good if you wish to prevent people from feeling sad.

Does this suggest all dark colors are bad? No. You need to determine what colors you like and what colors you need to stay away from when decorating. After doing this, you could paint freely, understanding you are creating a space you can genuinely call home.

Prominent Colors

If you have an interest in home decorating utilizing color, here are certain prominent color choices and their meanings. You could choose to paint your whole home a uniform color, or paint area by area.

Bear in mind that subtle distinctions in color might have a profound impact on how you respond to color, so make sure you "test-drive" a color prior to painting your walls.

You could do this by going to a neighborhood home improvement shop and getting a couple of swatches of color. Additionally, you can purchase a little color can you believe you want and paint a little area, or one wall, and see how you respond to it.

-Red-- if you wish to develop an enthusiastic environment, one loaded with energy, heat or power, red could be an excellent color. Many individuals alternate shades of red or red colors with abundant cream colors when painting their bedrooms. Bear in mind, nevertheless, for some red additionally inspires sensations of irritation or hostility, so make sure to determine your reaction prior to painting.

-Yellow-- this color normally inspires happiness, joy, favorable feelings, a feeling of freshness or clean, hope, and reminds individuals of the sunlight. Yellow can likewise imply something harmful or dangerous to some individuals. You might think about a pale shade to counter this impact.

-Blue-- this is an outstanding color to bring peace and serenity into any room in your house. It might likewise work as a hunger suppressant, so you may consider it for your kitchen area if you wish to stay in shape and trim. Certain individuals find darker blue tones depressing.

-Orange-- this color, such as yellow, is loaded with vibrancy and energy. It is an excellent color if you desire a productive and lively home.

-Green-- this is likewise a nurturing color and many find it calming. Some think it brings good fortune and for others, it signifies a more natural environment or nature. Nevertheless, green can likewise signify "envy" or jealousy, so track your sensations around this color.

-White-- there are numerous white shades. If you choose pure white, you might inspire sensations of purity, or you might inspire a hospital or clinical environment, so be weary of the shade of white you utilize. Lots of people find that white color signifying inner peace and a feeling of humbleness. In certain cultures, white represents death. Think about the white lily, a stunning white flower typically used throughout funerals. Be weary of your beliefs and response regarding this color when decorating.

Encertain you test drive these colors. Take a look at the colors above. Spend a bit of time with every color. Purchase fabrics of these colors and choose which colors you take pleasure in the most, and what energy they supply you with.

This is going to assist you when you choose colors to paint the areas of your home.

Positioning of Objects in the Home

How you position or where you position items in your room impacts your environment. The majority of people think it is ideal to create open spaces where you are able to walk freely.

More than once, we discussed how essential it is to get rid of clutter when you can. In Feng Shui, the objective of putting things is to promote the motion of energy, referred to as "chi" in any room. This brings favorable sensations and prosperity.

Here are certain simple actions you could take to create a reasonable, functional and beneficial circulation in your living space:

Ensure all walkways are roomy, and open so you feel you have more area and do not trip on things.

Do not obstruct doors, and make sure they can open easily to enable heat and success into your home.

Avoid clutter in any part of the home as this could generate sensations of mayhem or a disorganized environment. It could likewise obstruct favorable energy.

Attempt to permit air to stream easily through rooms, utilizing ventilation or by uncovering or unclogging windows.

Avoid putting a bed straight across from a door or mirror as this can disrupt your natural sleep cycle or rhythms according to some.

Make certain mirrors reflect favorable or visually enticing things, so when you look at them you feel relaxed and tranquil.

Utilize plants to design an environment loaded with animation and life, and to supply a feeling of calm when operating in a stressful environment.

Feng Shui is frequently extremely methodical in its nature. Individuals study Feng Shui for several years prior to mastering the art of developing a favorable and energetically balanced environment. Simply bear in mind, your goal is to develop an area YOU feel comfy in. You might find putting your couch on one side of a room, for instance, brings you more happiness than putting it on another.

Constantly utilize your instinct when putting things throughout your home, and odds are you are going to develop your home pleasingly. You might find you put items and move them often up until you develop a comfy workplace. This is completely normal. You might likewise discover with time that you have a requirement to alter the way things are put in your home. Do what you feel is appropriate at the time, and you can't fail.

Some state when it pertains to Feng Shui, it is ideal to make tiny adjustments initially, so you are able to observe how your body responds.

If for instance, you paint a room, move your couch and put a brand-new fountain in a corner on the identical day, and feel different, how could you be certain if all or one of these caused your sensations?

When decorating and moving things around to enhance the circulation of energy, make certain you take the time. This is the ideal method to generate a peaceful and tranquil environment. If you want, reorganize the furnishings in your home and walkways numerous times, to make certain the interior shows your real character, desires and wishes.

If you wish to find out more about developing a favorable and roomy environment, have a look at a couple of books on Feng Shui from the library. You could likewise Google the term and discover a plethora of information on the internet.

Professional Design Tips

Now that you have a fundamental understanding of what style is all about, it is time to evaluate some methods to bring your home together. You must constantly work to create a house that appears balanced. You do not wish to decorate your home so that you feel you reside in a disorderly environment. You could quickly decorate and produce a favorable balance by following the methods laid out in this part.

You know you can purchase affordable pieces to furnish your home. You can likewise blend and match. One secret to developing a pleasant environment is to purchase a couple of essential pieces you like, even if they are costly, and complement the remainder of the area you intend to decorate with basic items which cost a lot less.

Blending and matching work well as long as you have some style aspects in mind. For instance, if you wish to blend antique furnishings with some modern pieces, you can do so, simply ensure the pieces match each other somehow or match the general design you wish to generate within your home.

Decorating for Success

If you take a look at interior design, there are 2 major methods to decorate. You could keep things tidy, straightforward and structured (as one may if they wished to utilize the concepts of Feng Shui), or you could make a natural, positive and abstract environment which fits your character.

Some individuals choose to utilize exotic or enjoyable pieces throughout their houses to develop an amusing and dynamic environment. Others wish to develop a tranquil and peaceful environment. Still, others purchase pieces showing their cultural heritage. No single method is the proper way, since everybody is different. How you decorate should reflect who you are and how you feel.

You might discover you want an exotic style or design in the family area or the bedroom, yet serene and well balanced in the living or home office area. You could blend and match, though the majority of people have a tendency to stick to one style or another. The secret to your success is your capability to have an open mind, and have a good time.

Make certain you do not utilize a lot of pieces when designing. In case you have a plan to place family photos along a corridor, for instance, as a method to embellish your walls, do so, however, do it simply.

Attempt utilizing the identical frame design for all the pictures you utilize. If you blend and match a lot of various designs, you are going to create a disorderly looking environment.

Candles Décor

Some individuals decorate with color and candles alone. Candles can be found in lots of sizes, shapes, colors and aromas. You can purchase little tea candles for less than a buck, or bigger candles for 10. You could utilize candles to accessorize or candle lamps to replace artificial lighting in your house. If you desire an eco-friendly home, you might wish to purchase organic candles.

The trick to making candles work is discovering appropriate holders. These you can discover anywhere. You could purchase sets of candleholders and utilize them to decorate a whole home, and save cash by buying more instead of less.

Simply ensure if you intend to light candles, you substitute them routinely. Tea candles are ideally utilized as lighting sources due to the fact that they are affordable. You do not wish to purchase a $200 ornamental candle and light it, needing to replace it month-to-month. That gets costly.

On the other hand, you could utilize the bigger piece as décor, and light tea candles to enable a pleasing radiance and aroma. Many people discover a mix of methods creates simply the appropriate feel and look for their home. One word of warning - If you do purchase candles, make certain you buy candles which have safeguards. You do not wish to burn down your wonderfully decorated home. Always ensure you extinguish candles when you are finished with utilizing them.

If you are sensitive to scent, attempt utilizing unscented candles. Numerous candles come in powerful scents, so make certain you examine the candle's components BEFORE you purchase, so you do not cause an allergy when decorating your house.

As you continue to utilize your creativity and embrace brand-new methods, you are going to discover new ideas that motivate you to alter the feel and look of your home. When this occurs, return to your goal-setting list and develop brand-new goals for your house. Eventually, this is going to enable you to develop a skillfully created home whenever you desire, without investing a fortune.

I hope that you enjoyed reading through this book and that you have found it useful. If you want to share your thoughts on this book, you can do so by leaving a review on the Amazon page. Have a great rest of the day.

Printed in Great Britain
by Amazon

68077189R00050